INTERLAKEN PICTURE BOOK

Capturing the Charm and Beauty of Interlaken in a Stunning Picture Book (High quality photos)

Bonita Green

Amazing photos of Interlaken

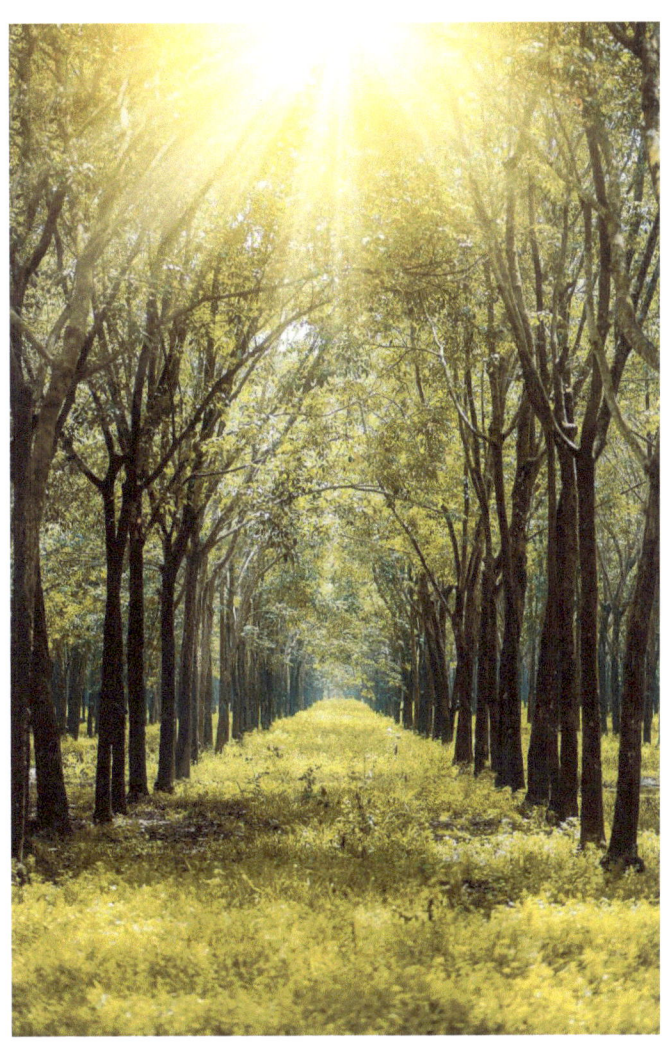

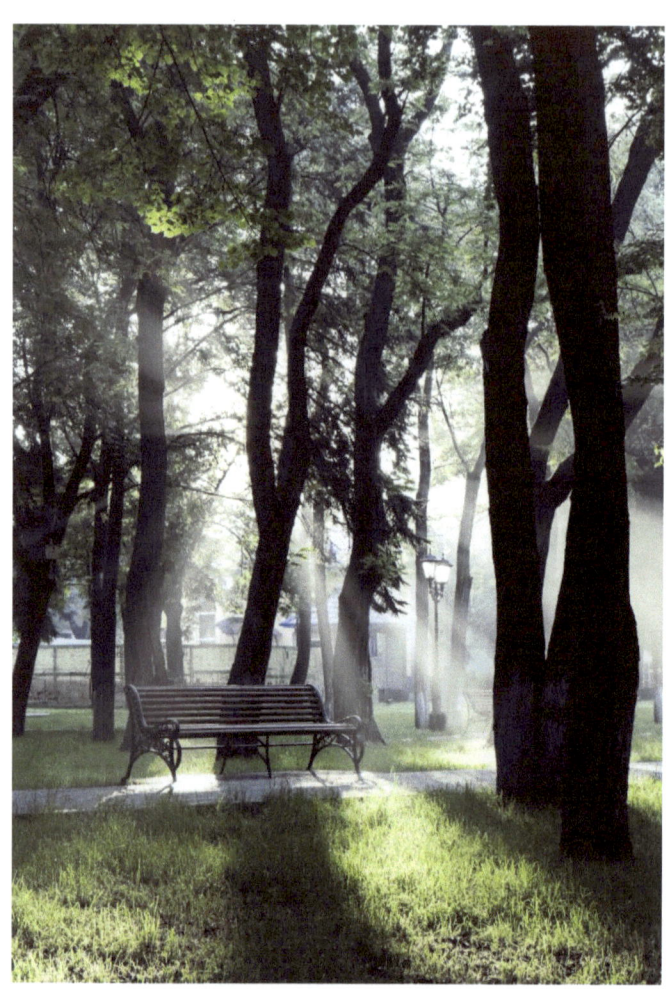

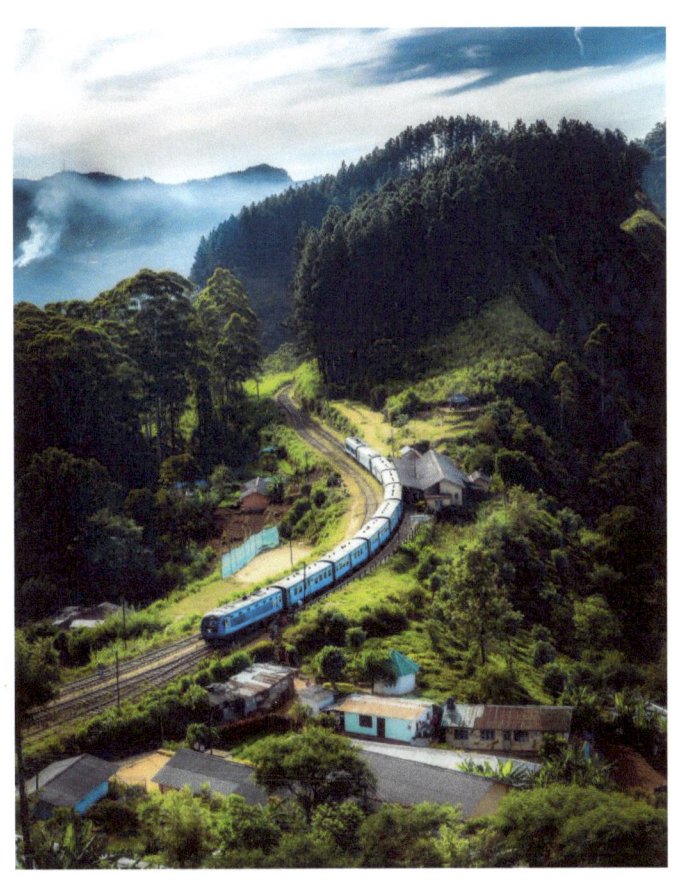

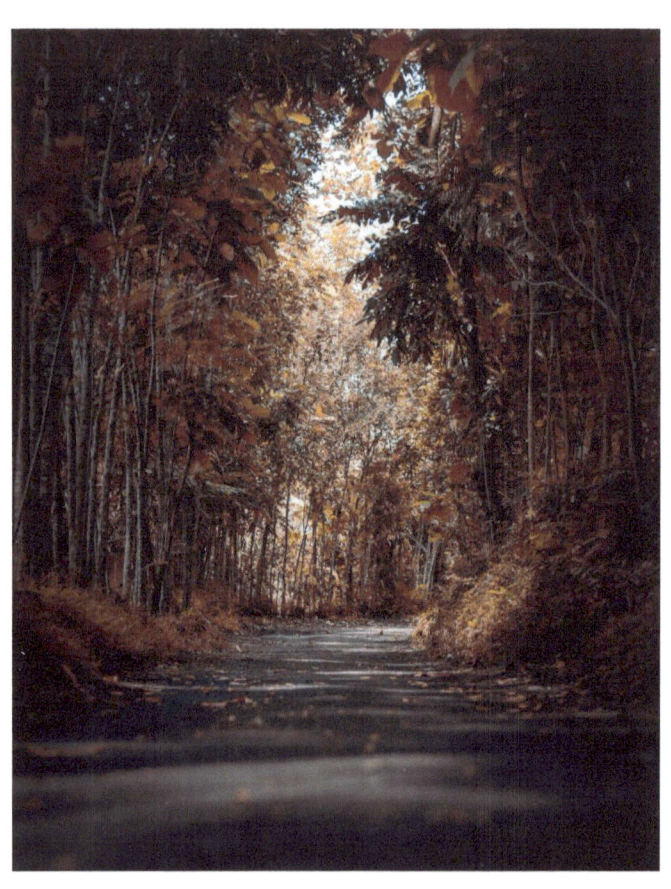

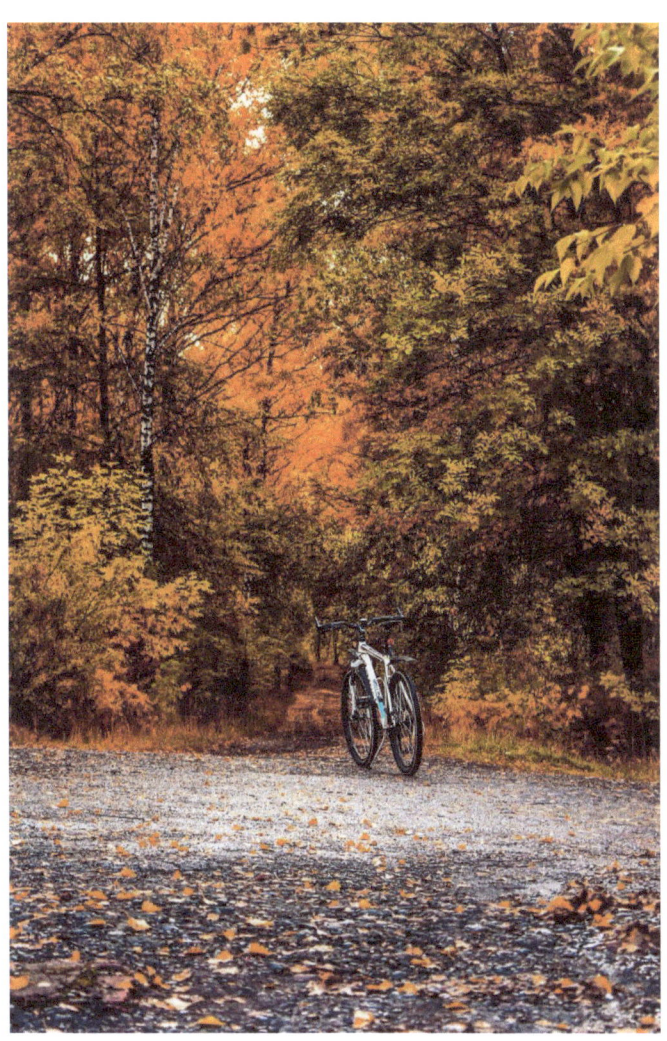

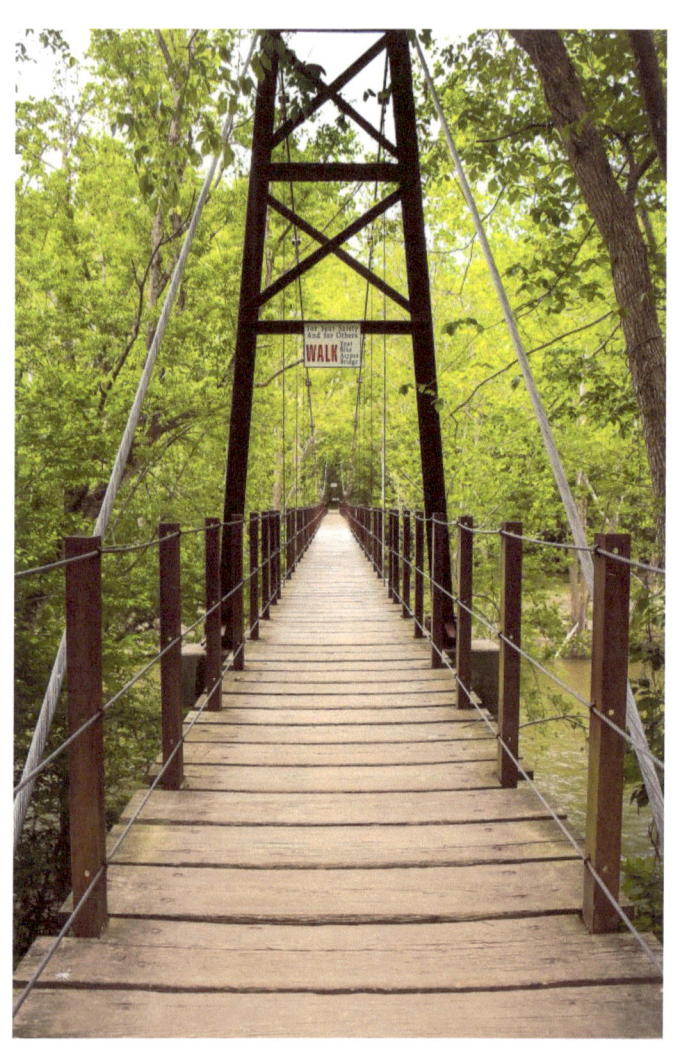

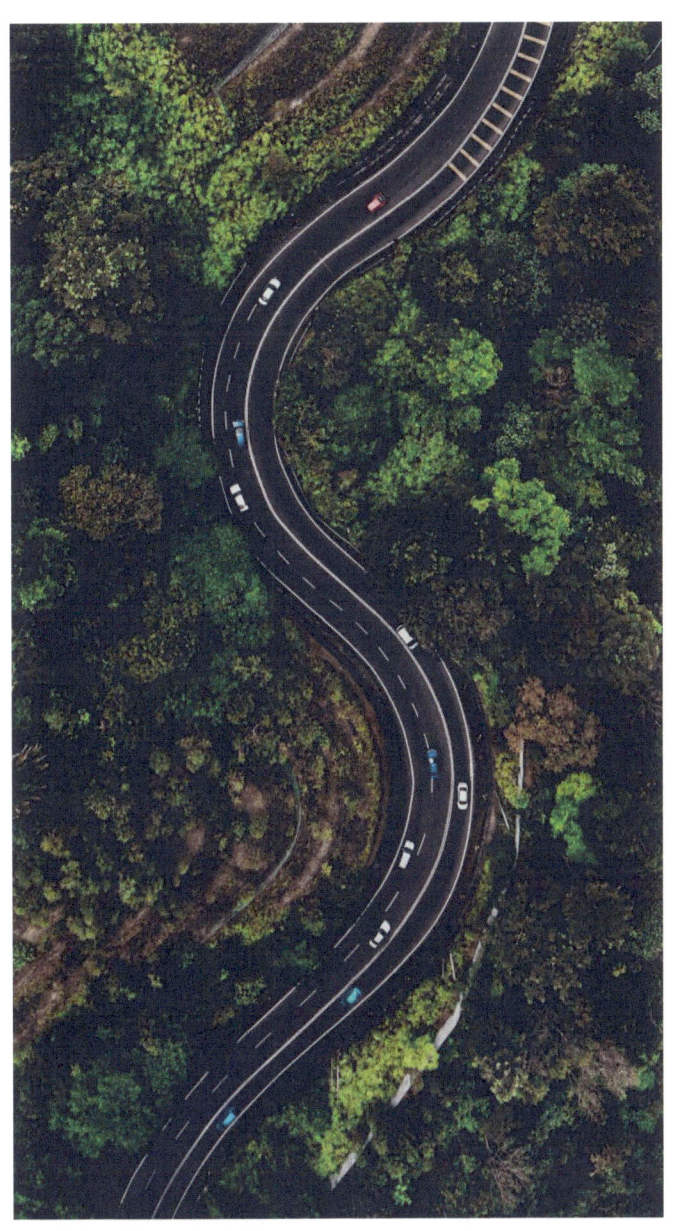

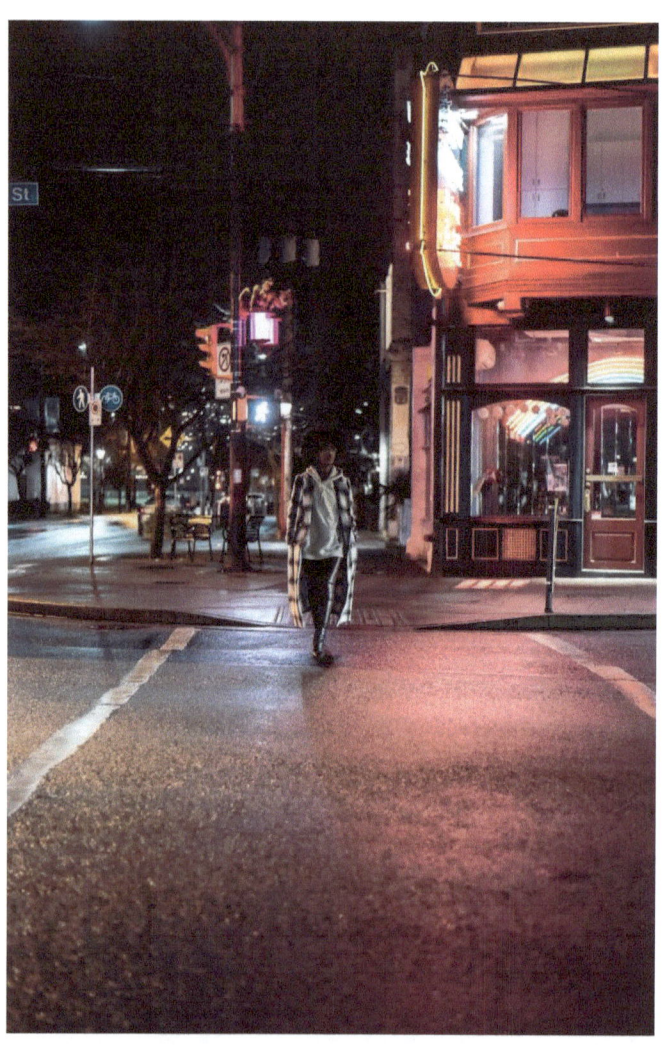

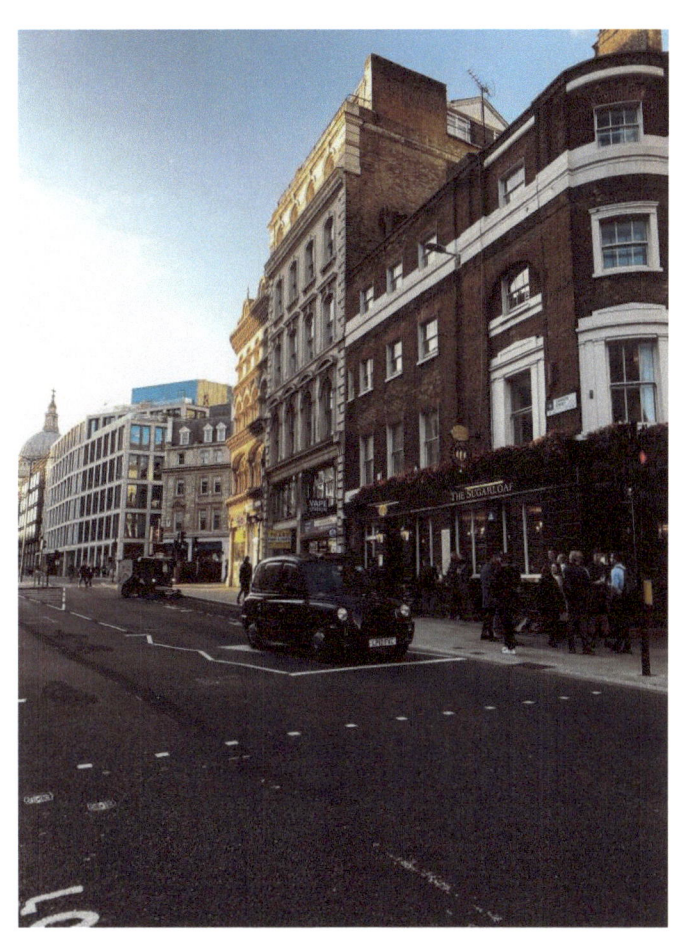

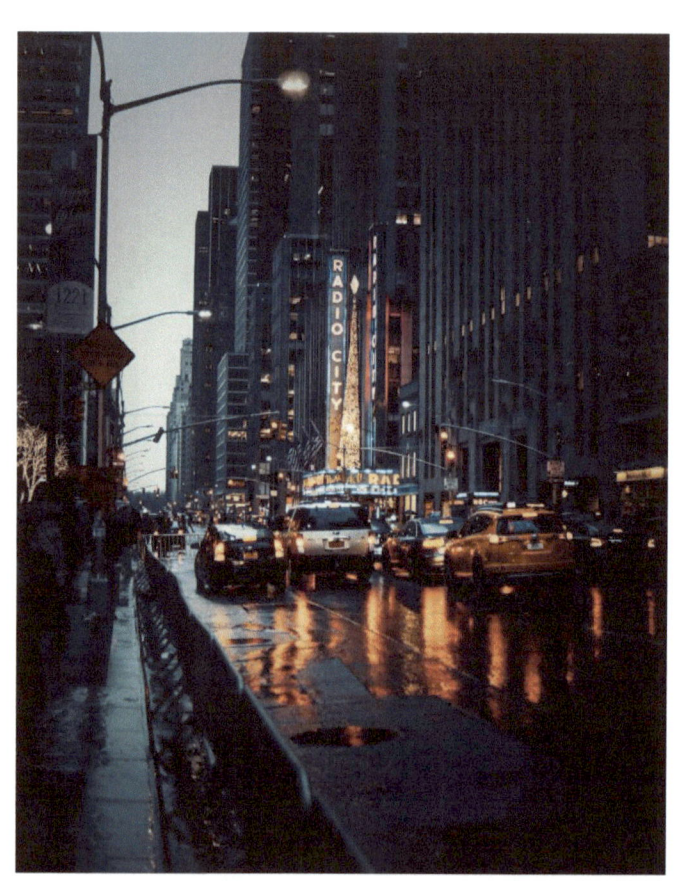

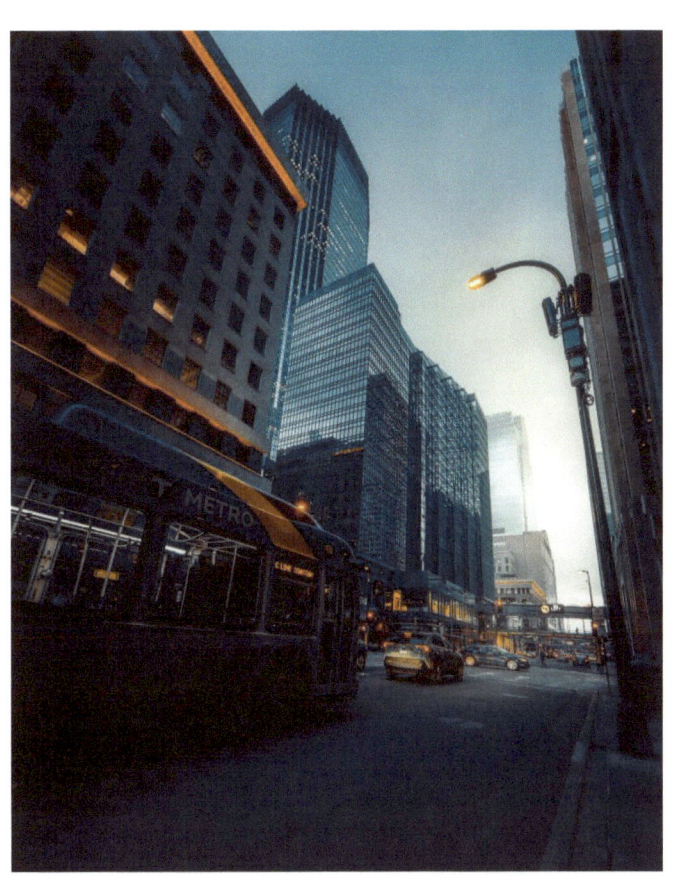

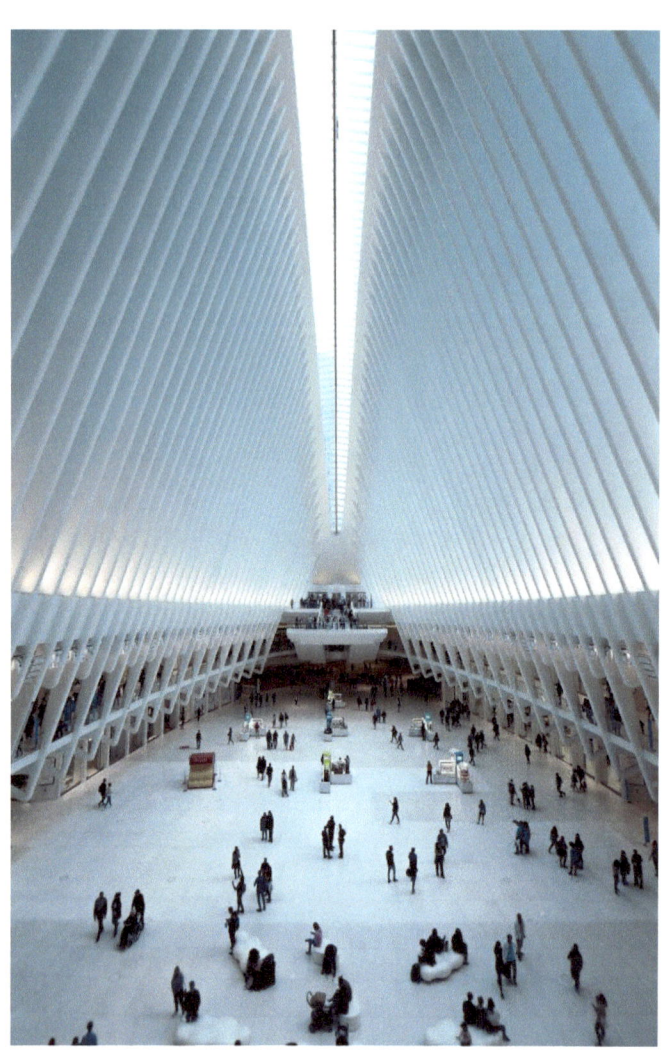

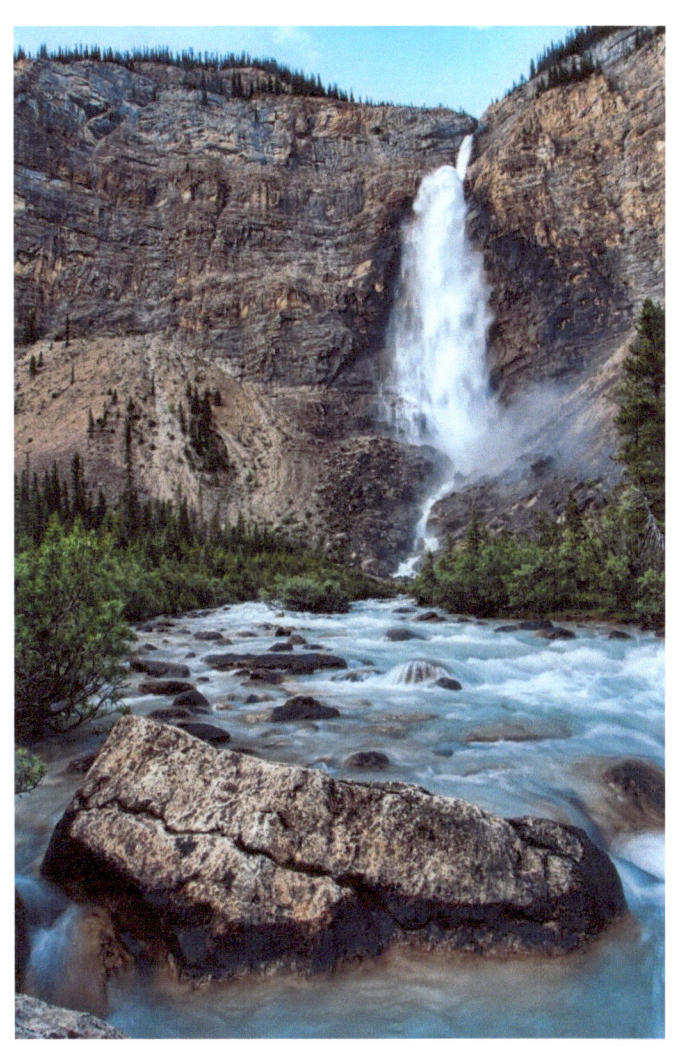

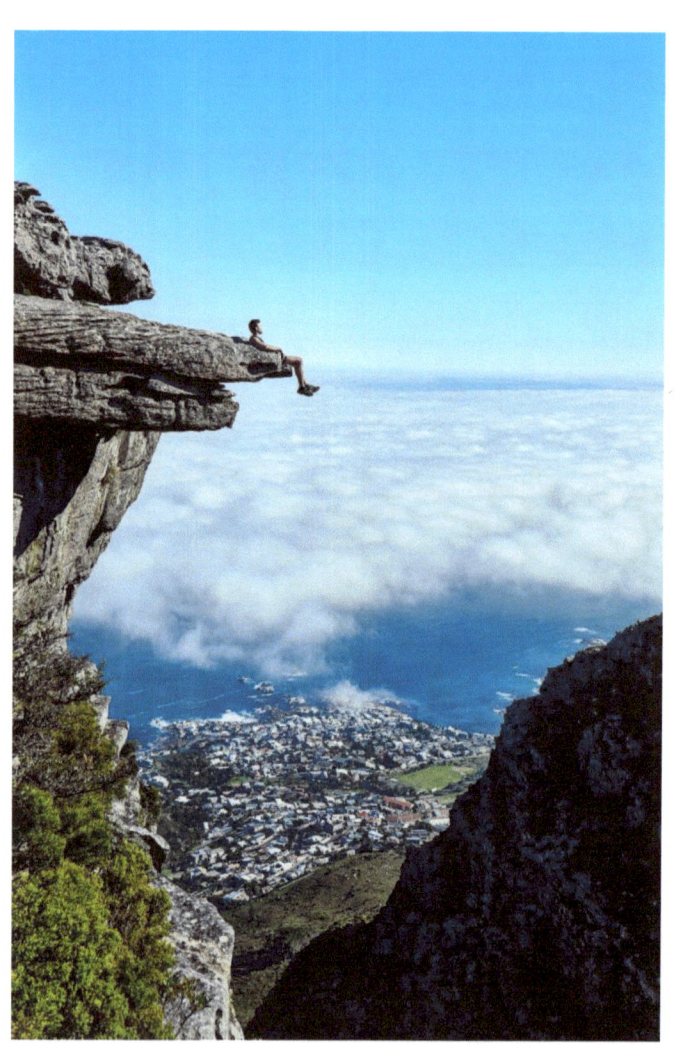

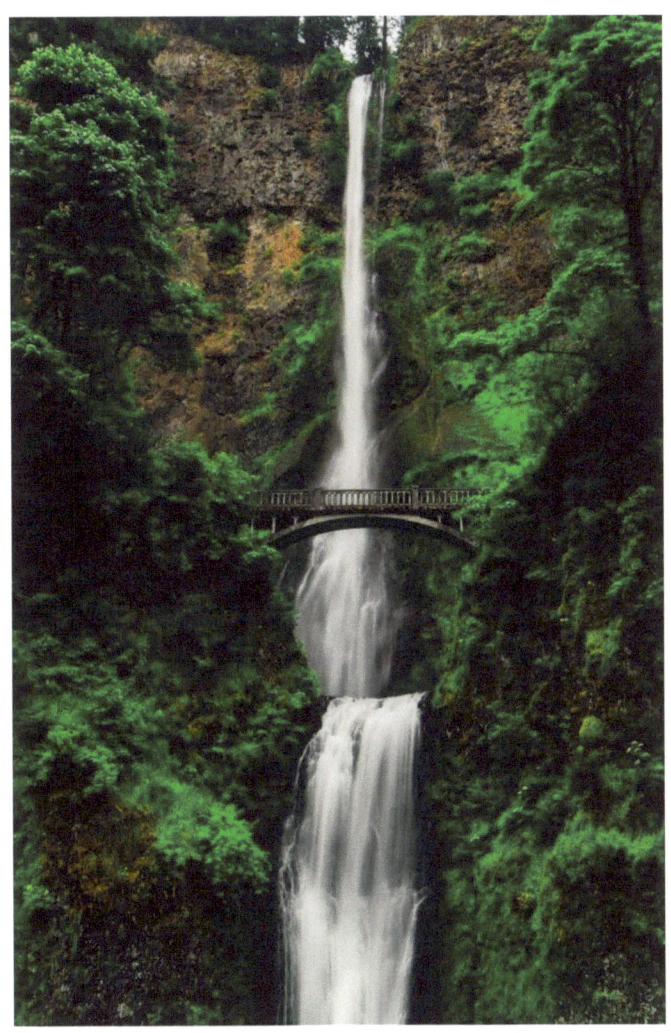

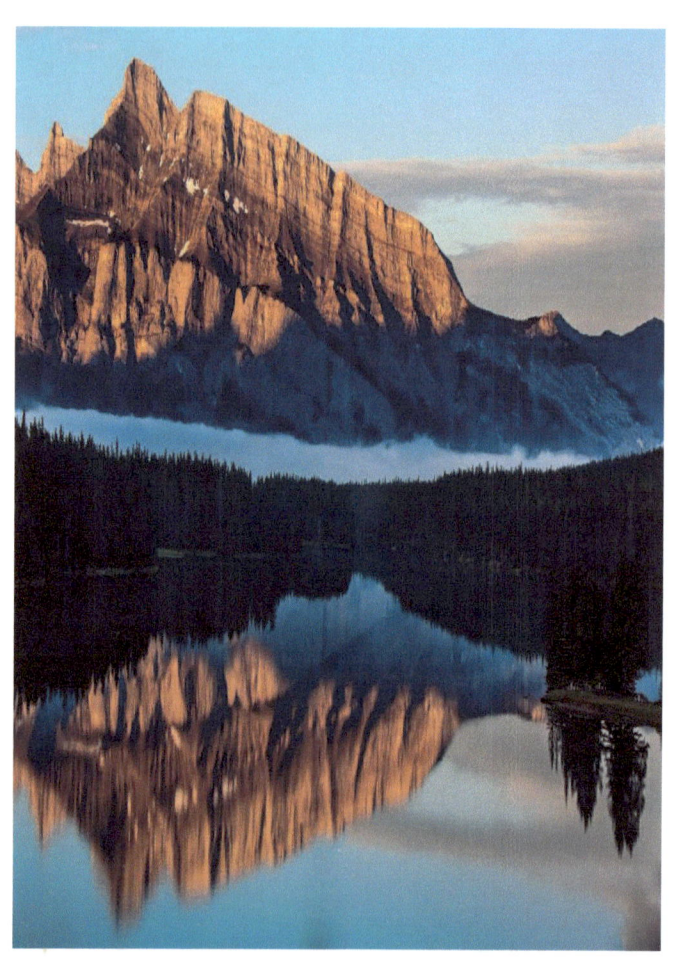

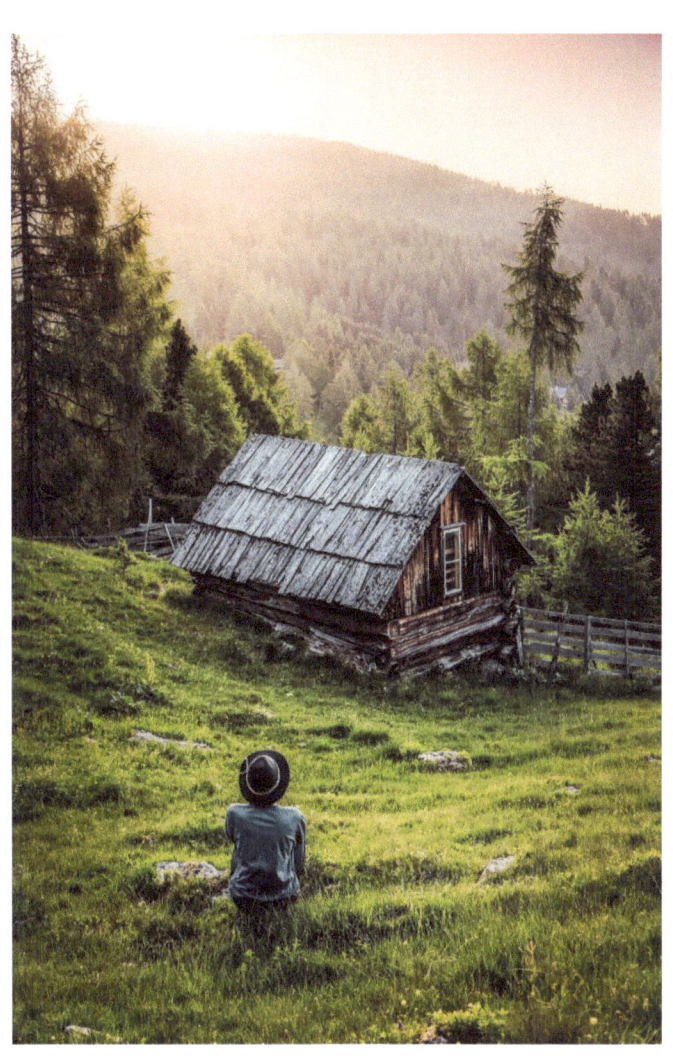

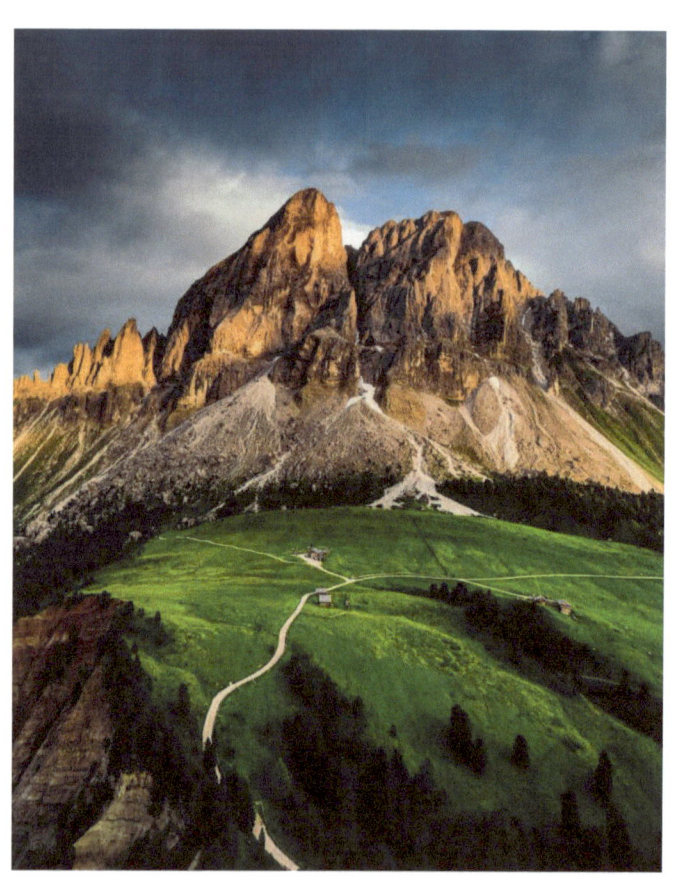

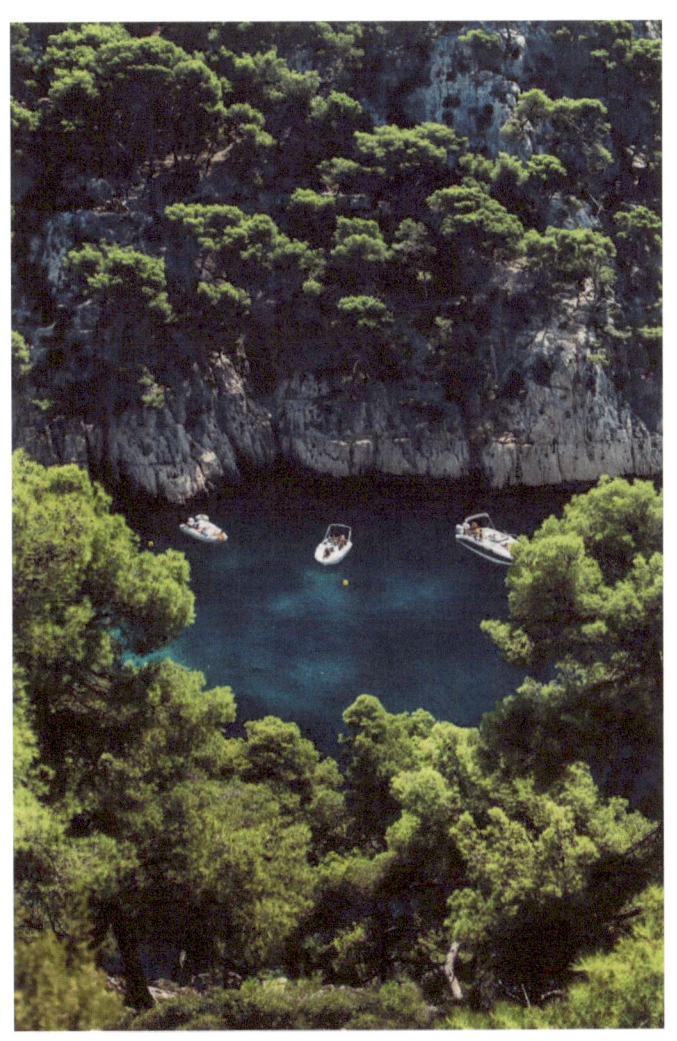

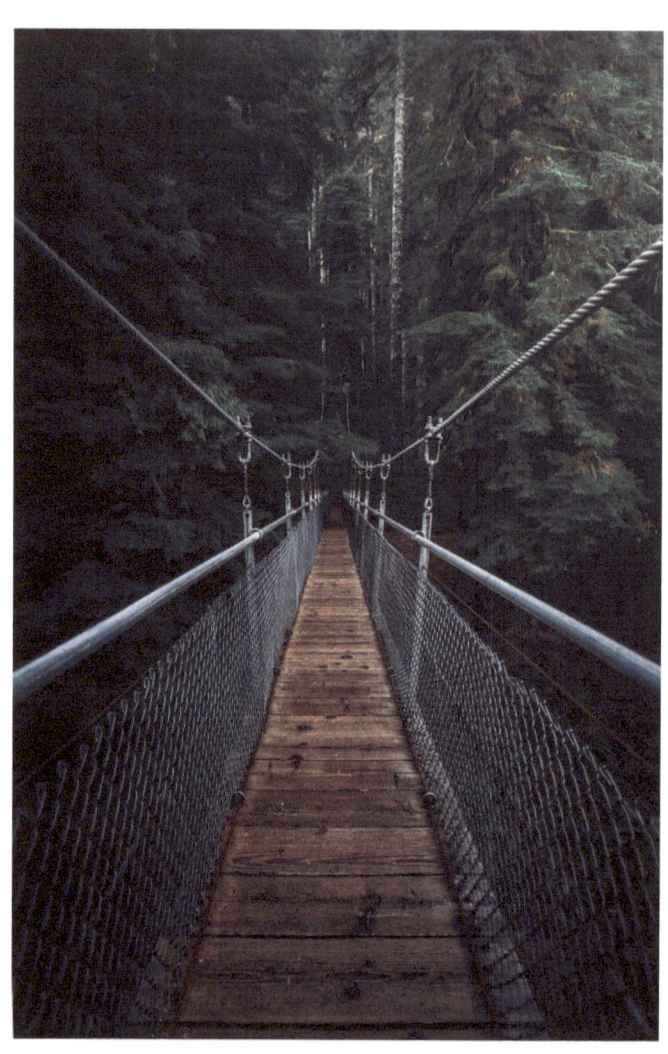

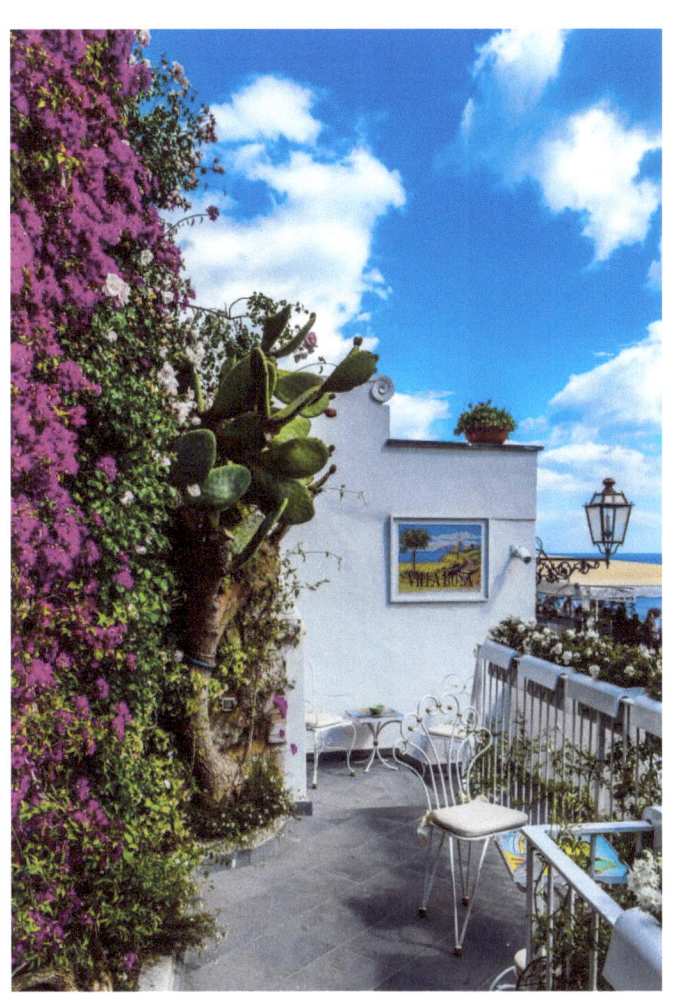

Travel Planner

Destination (s)	When

Expenses	Budget	Actual

Transportation		
Hotel		
Food		
Shopping		
Gifts		

Total		

Places to see

- _____

- _____

- _____

- _____

Places to eat

- _____

- _____

- _____

- _____

● _____

Places to shop

● _____

● _____

● _____

● _____

● _____

Emergency contacts

- _____

- _____

- _____

- _____

- _____

Addresses of places I'm staying at

- _____

- _____

- _____

- _____